Ron Fry's
HOW TO STUDY
Program

Improve
Your
Reading

Ron Fry's
HOW TO STUDY
Program

Improve
Your
Reading

By
Ron Fry

THE CAREER PRESS
180 Fifth Ave.
PO Box 34
Hawthorne, NJ 07507
1-800-CAREER-1
201-427-0229 (outside U.S.)
FAX: 201-427-2037

/ Ron Fry

Ron Fry's **HOW TO STUDY** *Program:*
Improve Your Reading
ISBN 0-934829-90-X, $4.95

Cover design by Dean Johnson Design, Inc.

Chapter 2, pp. 23-27, adapted from **FROM CAMPUS TO CORPORATION and the next ten years,** copyright © 1990 Drs. Stephen Strasser and John Sena, pp. 73-81. Used with permission.

Copies of this volume may be ordered by mail or phone directly from the publisher. To order by mail, please include price as noted above, $2.50 handling per order, and $1.00 for each book ordered. Send to: The Career Press, Inc., 180 Fifth Ave., P.O. Box 34, Hawthorne, N.J. 07507

Or call Toll-free 1-800-CAREER-1 (in Canada: 201-427-0229) to order using your VISA or MasterCard or for further information on all books published or distributed by The Career Press.

Table of Contents

Improve Your Reading

Read On! It Might Even Be Fun

I know, I know. This book is just what you need—*another* treatise on the value of reading, *another* stack of pages to wade through—in addition to the science, math, history and English texts you *already* have to read.

Don't be fooled by the title (or the fact that maybe your parents gave it to you). I think you'll find this is a book unlike any you've read before. And if you take the time to read it, I promise it will make the *rest* of that stack of reading a lot easier to get through.

Why? Because I'm going to show you how to plow through *all* your reading assignments—whatever the subjects—better and faster...*and* how to remember *more* of what you've read.

This book is *not* a gimmicky speed-reading method. It's not a spelling and grammar guide. Nor is it a lecture on the joys of reading. It's a *practical* guide, geared to *you*—a student who isn't necessarily a poor reader, but who wants to get more from your academic reading—whether texts or the classics—and do better in school.

Personally, I love to read: the classics, spy thrillers, science fiction, sports magazines, the newspaper, the back of the cereal box...I'll even admit to skimming through a paperback romance while waiting for the dentist a couple of weeks ago.

But, believe me, just because I loved to read didn't mean it was easy for me to face some of those deadly textbook reading assignments. As a student, you inevitably will be required, as I was, to spend hours poring through ponderous, fact-filled, convoluted reading assignments for subjects that are required but not exactly up there on the "All-Time Favorites" list.

You may love reading for pleasure, but have trouble reading textbook assignments for certain subjects. You may get the reading done, but forget what you've read nearly as quickly as you read it. Or you just may hate the thought of sitting still to read *anything*. What*ever* kind of student you are—and what*ever* your level of reading skill—I've written this book to help you surmount your reading challenge, *whatever it may be.*

You'll learn what you *should* read—and what you don't *have* to. You'll discover how to cut down on the time you spend reading. How to identify the main idea in your reading, as well as the important details. How to remember more of what you read.

I'll show you different ways to read various types of books, from dry science texts to cumbersome classics.

Who knows? I might even convince you reading is fun!

Chapter 1

Welcome To The Adventure

Reading is an adventure, when you go with the poets into the realms of fancy and imagination; you see life with the novelist; you go down to the sea in ships and unto the ends of the earth with great explorers; the scientist takes you into the laboratory; in biography you are let into the mystery of men's lives; the historian reconstructs the past and gives you glimpses of the future, and the philosopher gives you a glimpse of his wisdom.
— Holbrook Jackson, *The Joy Of Reading*

You're probably *not* reading this book because you agree with Mr. Jackson that reading is an adventure. At best, reading is something you *do*, not something you *love*. At worst, it is a necessary torture to be endured with the same grim-jawed determination as a root canal.

(I don't mean to impugn your study skills, but if you just adored reading, I doubt you'd be reading this book!)

In any case, you must come to realize the vital place reading has in life—and not just in school. We live in what has been called the Information Age—the electronic media bombards our senses with all sorts of sound and picture bytes. But no matter how technologically advanced our society becomes—how large "big-screen" TVs grow, how small Sony radios shrink—reading is and always will be an essential skill.

And the *better* you read, the more you'll learn and the more you'll be able to become (and the more electronic playthings you'll be able to afford!).

When you're a *good* reader, the world really is your oyster—you qualify for better schools, better jobs, better pay. Poor readers qualify for poor jobs and less fulfilling lives.

Ready to begin? Get motivated!

Any attempt to improve your reading must begin with motivation. Reading is not a genetic trait that is written in your DNA—there's no gene that makes you a good or bad reader like the ones that decide your hair or eye color. For the most part, reading is an *acquired* skill. A skill *you* can secure, grow and sharpen.

You just have to *want* to. This adventure Mr Jackson describes is reserved for those who will invest the time and energy necessary to become good readers—for those of you sufficiently motivated to do so.

Within this book, I will address a number of very practical techniques that are sure to increase your reading comprehension. But they are just *techniques.*

You'll invariably find them utterly useless if you are not motivated to read in the first place.

As the Nike commercial lambastes all of us weekend warriors—"Just Do It!" This attitude—not technique—is where the quest for improved reading begins. You must make reading a habit.

Good reader vs. poor reader

Look at the following comparison of a good reader and a poor reader as if you were some corporate hot shot who could hire just one of the individuals:

> **Good Reader:** You read for purpose. You've clearly defined your reason for reading—a question you want answered, facts you must remember, ideas you need to grasp, current events that affect you, or just the pleasure of following a well-written story.
> **Poor Reader:** Yes, you read, but often have no real reason for doing so. You aimlessly struggle through assigned reading, with little effort to grasp the "message."

> **Good Reader:** You read and assimilate thought. You hear and digest the concepts and ideas that are communicated.
> **Poor Reader:** You get lost in the muddle of words, struggling to make sense of what the author is trying to say. You are often bored out of your skull because you force yourself to read every word to "get the message"... which you don't.

> **Good Reader:** You read critically and ask questions to evaluate whether the author's arguments are reasonable or off the wall. You recognize biases and don't just "believe" everything you read.

Poor Reader: You swallow everything you read—hook, line and sinker. You suffer from the delusion that everything in print is true, and are easily swayed from what you formerly believed to be true by any argument that sounds good.

Good Reader: You read a variety of books, magazines, and newspapers—not limiting your reading to the most current "Far Side" humor book. You enjoy all types of reading —fiction, poetry, biography, current events.

Poor Reader: You're a one-track reader— you read the sports pages, comics or Gothic novels. Current events? You catch updates about your world from occasional TV news "sound bites."

Good Reader: You enjoy reading and embrace it as an essential tool in your desire to better yourself.

Poor Reader: You hate to read, deeming it a chore to be endured only when you have to. Reading is "boring."

Take a minute and ask yourself, who would *you* hire? Yes, you might hire Mr. Poor Reader...in some low-paying job. But would you ever put someone with such low-level skills in a responsible position?

At this point, I won't ask you to evaluate your own level of reading skills. Characterizing yourself as a "good" or "poor" reader was not the point of this exercise. What is important is to realize that Ms. Good Reader didn't spring full-blown from Zeus's cranium reading Shakespearean sonnets and quoting Winston Churchill. She learned to read the same way you and I did—with "See Spot run."

In time and through making reading a habit, Ms. Good Reader acquired and honed a skill that will open a world of opportunity to her.

Mr. Poor Reader, at some point, decided that being a good reader was not worth the effort and made *poor* reading his habit.

The good news is that being a poor reader is not a life sentence—you *can* improve your reading. The challenge is to find the motivation!

How to remember less...faster

Retention is primarily a product of what you understand. It has little to do with how *fast* you read, how great an outline you can construct or how many fluorescent colors you can mark your textbooks with. Reading a text, grasping the message and remembering it, are the fundamentals that make for high-level retention. Reading at a 1,000-word-per-minute clip does not necessarily mean that you have a clue as to what a text really says.

Do you read so slowly that you think a speed-reading course may be necessary? Reading for speed has some merit—many people who are slow readers read as little as possible, simply because they find it so tedious and boring. But just reading faster is not the answer to becoming a good reader.

(If you find yourself reading every word in a text every time you read something, you probably *would* benefit from some type of speed reading help. But if you are already relatively adept at skimming and sight reading long passages, a speed reading course would do little to help you *retain* more of what you read.)

As you work toward improving your reading, realize that, in the race for retention, speed is secondary to comprehension. If you can read an assignment faster than anyone in class, but couldn't give a one-sentence synopsis of what you read, you lose. But if you really "get the message" of the author—even if it takes you an hour or two longer than some of your friends—your time will pay off in huge dividends in the classroom, and later in life.

That's why this book concentrates only on how you as a student can increase what you retain from your reading assignments. Whether you're reading a convoluted textbook that bores even the professor to tears or a magazine article, newspaper feature, or novel, you follow a certain process in order to absorb what you've read, which consists of:

1. Grasping the main idea
2. Gathering the facts
3. Figuring out the sequence of events
4. Drawing conclusions

When you spend an hour reading an assignment, then can't recall what you've just read, it's usually because a link in this chain has been broken. You've skipped one of these crucial steps in your reading process, leaving your understanding of the material filled with gaps.

To increase your retention rate, you need to master *each level* in this chain of comprehension. Not everything you read will require that you comprehend on all four levels. Following a set of cooking directions, for example, simply requires that you discern the sequence for adding all ingredients. Other reading will demand that you are able to compile facts, identify a thesis and give some critical thought as to its validity.

Ms Good Reader is not only able to perform at each level of comprehension, but also has developed an instinct: She recognizes that certain things she reads can be read *just* to gather facts or *just* to grasp the main idea. She then is able to read quickly to accomplish this goal and move on to her next assignment—or to that Steven King novel she's been dying to read.

This book will help you develop a sense of what is involved in *each* step of the reading process.

The first chapters will address these different steps and provide exercises designed to help you master each stage in the process of retaining what you read.

In the final chapters, we will look at how to read literature, how to read a math or science textbook and how to outline so that you can easily review a text.

By the time you finish this short book, you should find that by following the procedures I've suggested, you have significantly improved your reading comprehension.

Chapter 2

Reading With Purpose

Even if you consider yourself "not much of a reader," you read *something* every day: A magazine article, the instructions for hooking up the VCR, telephone messages tacked on the refrigerator, notes from your latest heart-throb.

Regardless of *what* you are reading, you have a purpose that dictates *how* you are going to read it—and you read different items in different ways. You wouldn't read the VCR instructions as you would a novel, any more than you'd read the magazine article in the same way as a grocery list. Without a purpose, you'd find yourself reading aimlessly and very inefficiently.

Unfortunately, many of the students I've talked to haven't realized the importance of having a purpose for reading. Their lack of reading purpose can be summed up by the proverb, "If you aim at nothing, you will hit the bullseye every time."

Before you can understand what you're reading—and *remember* it—you must know *why* you're reading it in the first place.

Defining your purpose for reading

What is your purpose in reading? If the best answer you can come up with is, "Because my teacher said so," we need to do a little work to come up with some better reasons. Reading a chapter just so you can say, "I finished my assignment," is relatively futile. You may as well put the book under a pillow and hope to absorb it by osmosis.

Unless you identify some purpose to read, you will find yourself flipping the pages of your textbooks while seldom retaining anything more than the chapter titles.

According to reading experts, there are six fundamental purposes for reading:

1. To grasp a certain message
2. To find important details
3. To answer a specific question
4. To evaluate what you are reading
5. To apply what you are reading
6. To be entertained

Because reading with purpose is the first step toward improved comprehension, let me suggest some simple techniques you can use to identify a purpose for *your* textbook reading.

Find the clues in your textbook

Every textbook offers some clues that will help you define a purpose for reading. Begin with a very quick overview of the assignment, looking for questions that you'd like answered. Consider the following elements of your reading assignment *before* you begin your reading.

Much like the headlines of a newspaper clue you into what the story is about, these elements will give you an insight into what the section or chapter is trying to communicate:

1. Chapter heads and subheads

Chapter titles and bold-faced subheads announce the detail about the main topic. And, in some textbooks, paragraph headings or bold-face "lead-ins" announce that the author is about to provide finer details.

So start each reading assignment by going through the chapter, beginning to end, *reading* only *the bold-faced heads and subheads.*

For example, suppose you encountered the heading, "The Demise of the American Indian," in your history text. You might use it to form the following questions:

A. *What* caused the demise of the American Indian?

B. *Who* caused the demise of the American Indian?

C. *When* did the demise of the Indian occur?

As you read the chapter, you'll find yourself seeking answers to these questions. You now have a purpose!

Often you may find headings that have words or terms you don't recognize. Seeking to define these terms or explain a concept should then define your purpose.

This process of headline reading takes only a few minutes, but it lays the groundwork for a more intelligent and efficient reading of the chapter. You'll have some idea where the author is headed, which will give you a greater sense of what the most important details are. And clarify where you should be concentrating your studying.

2. End-of-chapter summaries

If you read a mystery from start to finish, the way the author hopes you will, you're likely to get thrown off the scent by "red herrings" and other common detective novel devices. However, if you read the last page first, knowing the outcome will help you detect how the author constructed the novel and built an open-and-shut case for his or her master sleuth. You'd perceive a wealth of details about the eventually unmasked murderer that might have gone *un*noticed had he been just another of the leading suspects.

Similarly, knowing what the author is driving at in a *textbook* will help you look for the important building blocks for his conclusions while you're reading.

It may not be fun to read a mystery novel this way, but when it comes to textbook reading, it will help you define your purpose for reading. And further, it will transform you into a much more *active* reader, making it less likely you'll doze off while being beaten senseless by the usual ponderous prose.

3. Pictures, graphs and charts

Most textbooks, particularly those in the sciences, will have charts, graphs, numerical tables, maps and other illustrations. All too many students see these as filler—padding to glace at quickly, and, just as quickly, forget.

If you're giving these charts and graphs short shrift, you're really shortchanging *yourself*. Be sure to observe how they supplement the text, what points they emphasize and make note of these.

4. Highlighted terms, vocabulary and other facts

In some textbooks, you'll discover that key terms and information are highlighted within the body text. (I don't mean highlighted by a previous student—consider such yellow-markered passages with caution!) To find the definitions of these terms, or to find the application of facts may then be your purpose for reading.

5. Questions

Some textbook publishers use a format in which key points are emphasized by questions, either within the body of or at the end of the chapter. If you read these questions *before* reading the chapter, you'll have a better idea of what material you need to pay closer attention to.

Prereading your assignment

If you begin your reading assignment by seeking out these heads, subheads and other purpose-finding elements of the chapter, you'll have completed your pre-reading step. What is pre-reading? It is simply beginning your assigned reading by reviewing these clues and defining your purpose (or purposes) for reading.

I advise that you *always* pre-read every assignment! Why? Have you ever spent the better part of an evening plowing through an assignment only to finish with little or no understanding of what you just read? If the answer is "Yes," then you probably failed to pre-read it.

Purpose defines reading method

Now let's look at how to use purpose to determine your *method* of reading. In most cases, your purpose for reading will dictate how you read.

There are basically three types of reading we all do:

1. *Quick reference reading* focuses on seeking specific information that addresses a particular question or concern we might have;

2. *Critical reading* involves discerning ideas and concepts that require a thorough analysis;

2. *Aesthetic or pleasure reading,* which we do for sheer entertainment or to appreciate an author's style and ability.

As you define your purpose for reading, you will determine which method of reading is necessary to accomplish this purpose. In the following table are some examples of types of reading, why you might read them and the method you should use:

What You're Reading	Purpose	Method
Newspaper advertisements	To locate best price for car	*Quick Reference*
Magazine	To stay aware of current events	*Quick Reference*
Self-help book	To learn to get along better with your family	*Critical*
Biology text	To prepare for an exam	*Critical*
New issue of *Rolling Stone*	To divert your attention from Biology!	*Pleasure*

If you're a good reader or desire to be one: You will always fit your reading *method* to your reading *purpose;* you have trained or are training yourself in a variety of reading skills; you have no problem switching your method to accommodate your purpose; and you are unsatisfied reading only one type of material.

A poor reader, on the other hand, reads everything the same way—plowing through the Biology assignment and the newspaper the same way...word by painful word. Reading with purpose is both foreign and forboding to such a person, which makes it difficult for him or her to adapt a method of reading.

Become an active reader

Reading with purpose is as vital to your comprehension and retention as oxygen is to life. Why? It is the cornerstone of *active* reading, reading that involves thinking—that process of engaging your mind and emotions in what the author is trying to communicate. Too many readers seek to absorb information passively as their eyes move across the page. The active reader *involves* him- or herself in receiving a message—a fact, an idea, an opinion—that is readily retained because he or she had a *purpose*.

Following is a passage adapted from **FROM CAMPUS TO CORPORATION and the Next Ten Years** by Drs. Stephen Strasser and John Sena. *Pre-read* the passage, in order to determine a *purpose* for reading. Be sure to use the note page following to jot down questions that may have been raised through your pre-read, and the purpose:

It has been described as a "rude awakening," "growing up," or "entering the real world." Regardless of the epithets, beginning employment at a new company constitutes a major change in your life.

Work starts *before* you start work

Immediately after your employer receives your letter of acceptance, call or visit your new boss and ask him or her to supply you with reading materials pertinent to your work. These may differ substantially from the documents that you used to prepare for your job interview. Sales reports, organizational charts, profit and loss statements, project assignments, account histories, technical information on company products, and the company handbook on policies and procedures will provide you with a much-needed context for understanding and discharging your new responsibilities.

If possible, ask your boss to suggest a coworker with whom you may meet to discuss nuts-and-bolts matters before your job begins. The first week on the new job is filled with so many distractions, that absorbing work-related information at that time is extremely difficult.

First-week distractions

1. Learning peoples' names, finding a parking space, registering pertinent information in the company's personnel system.
2. Meetings.
3. Finding a stapler, figuring out where to go for lunch, getting your word processor hooked up.
4. Meetings.
5. Introducing yourself to colleagues, wondering what your boss is really like, wondering what your boss's boss is really like.
6. Meetings.
7. Figuring out what and how much work to take home because you attended so many meetings, you couldn't get it all done.

Learn names

As soon as you are alone, write down the names and job titles of the people you meet. Addressing people by their names when you see them for the second time will please them, and will help you experience a sense of belonging.

Listen for how people address one another. Do coworkers, for instance, refer to each other by first names? Are bosses addressed by "Mr.," "Mrs." or "Ms.?" When are titles used?

Learn the culture of the firm

Companies, like people, have unique and distinctive personalities. Yours will have a certain value system, modes of acceptable and unacceptable behavior, systems of rewards and punishments, likes and dislikes, sacred cows and closet skeletons. The culture and personality of a firm must be understood before it is to be engaged or challenged.

Firms, like people, also have a negative side to their personalities. You will soon learn—whether you want to or not—about office romances, incompetent secretaries, boardroom backstabbings, office politics, and your boss's secret desire to build a sales pyramid in China. This "other," shadowy organization will slowly unfold before your eyes and ears. Allow this information to come to you; learn without getting personally involved. (You may wish to regard such information with a healthy skepticism.) By maintaining your distance from this darker side of the workplace, you will also maintain your credibility, integrity and job security.

Proceed cautiously

Don't expect to hit a home run during your first few weeks. Keep your eyes and ears open, ask questions selectively, and be a good listener. You should be courteous and amiable, but don't feel compelled to form intimate friendships after your first meeting with a person.

Be cautious about unburdening your soul, revealing your innermost thoughts. People often react negatively to this type of behavior, and may regard you with suspicion. A boss familiar with your personal problems, while sympathetic, may be reluctant to give you additional responsiblities—and the promotions that go with them.

Getting along with your boss

Learn to "read" what your boss wants. Does he or she like short or long explanations? Does he or she want to hear about all the problems, or only the major ones? Is he or she obsessive about punctuality and deadlines? Is he or she more approachable in the mornings or afternoons?

Learning a boss's *modus operandi* and idiosyncracies will help you become a more effective and valued employee.

Hold thy tongue

The desideratum in The ***Book of Common Prayer***, to keep "my tongue from evil-speaking... and slandering," is especially applicable in the workplace. In college, you could vociferously criticize professors and administrators with impunity. In the workplace, bad mouthing a superior is likely to bring your career to a crashing halt. Gossiping about a peer is just as bad.

Have realistic expectations

You may become resentful of your job soon after the excitement of having one wears off. This is not an unusual development. After all, this new job has radically altered your comfortable lifestyle. It has deprived you of much of your private time and left you with less control over your schedule.

While you may be convinced that you are not being appreciated rapidly enough, you may also be pulled in the opposite direction, suffereing from poignant pangs of insecurity and self-doubt.

Have realistic expectations of your job, your future and yourself during this demanding period. As a "junior person" you may well receive the worst assignments and be required to work long hours. All for what you consider little pay. Virtually all professionals serve an apprenticeship, and this should not be viewed as demeaning or unfair. Your apprenticeship is a time of rapid growth and development, and it is the foundation upon which you will build a successful career.

Summary

The unspoken rules covered in this chapter are unlikely to appear in your company handbook. But adhering to them is crucial to starting off on the right foot at your new job. Before you begin your job, and during your first weeks, make sure you've answered these questions for yourself:

1. How can I better prepare myself for my new job before I begin work?
2. How can I establish positive working relationships with my co-workers?
3. How can I make sure I perform as my boss wants me to?
4. How can I make sure not to offend my boss or co-workers?

Your Notes

What clues can you find that help you define a purpose for reading this passage?

_____

_____

_____

_____

_____

_____

What purpose or purposes did you determine for reading this passage?

_____

_____

_____

_____

_____

_____

What method, based on your purpose, would you use to read this passage?

_____

Chapter 3

Finding The Main Idea

In all good writing, there is a controlling thesis or message that connects all the specific details and facts. This concept or idea is usually expressed as a generalization that summarizes the entire text.

Good comprehension results when you are able to grasp this main message, even if you sometimes forget some of the details. When you understand the intent, you have a context in which to evaluate the reasoning, the attitude, and whether the evidence cited really is supportive of the conclusions drawn.

An obsession for facts alone can often obscure the "big picture," giving you an understanding of the trees but no concept of the forest. How many of you have spent hours studying your textbooks for an important exam, collecting dates and names and terms and formulas, but failed to ferret out the main idea, the underlying concept that is composed of these facts?

In longer, more involved readings, there are many messages that are combined to form a chain of thought, which, in turn, may or may not be communicating one thesis or idea.

Your ability to capture this chain of thought determines your level of comprehension—and what you retain.

Dissecting your reading assignment

To succeed in identifying the main idea in any reading assignment, you must learn to use these helpful tools:

1. The topic sentence of a paragraph
2. Summary sentences
3. Supporting sentences
4. Transitional statements

As you learn to dissect your reading assignment, paragraph by paragraph, identifying its many parts and their functions, you'll grasp the main idea much more quickly—and remember it much longer.

Recognizing a topic sentence

Every paragraph has a *topic sentence*—the sentence that summarizes what the paragraph is about. Even if a paragraph does not have such a clearly stated sentence, it can be implied or inferred from what is written.

Generally, the topic sentence is the first or last sentence of a paragraph—the one statement that announces, "Here's what this paragraph is all about!"

When the topic sentence is obscured or hidden, you may need to utilize two simple exercises to uncover it:

1. Pretend you're a headline writer for your local newspaper—write a headline for the paragraph you just read.
2. Write a five-word summary describing what the paragraph is about.

Exercise: Identifying the topic sentence

Write a headline or five-word summary for each of the following paragraphs:

> Manicuring and coloring the nails are not a recent beauty secret. Recent archaeology reveals that as early as 3200 B.C., the Chaldeans in Babylonia had gold manicure sets, meaning this practice is at least 5000 years old. Nefertiti and Cleopatra of ancient Egypt painted their fingernails and toenails for much the same reason women today paint theirs—to enhance their physical attractiveness. Historically it seems that cultured, upper-class women through the ages have deemed that coloring their nails is an important part of their effort to be beautiful.

> Baseball is an exciting game, especially when seen at the ballpark. Every year millions of fans don their baseball caps and head to the ballpark. Many of these same fans would argue that there is no better hot dog in the world than that consumed at a baseball game. In 1975, fans of the Boston Red Sox consumed 1.5 million hot dogs. With this kind of demand, the traditional method of boiling has been rendered obsolete

by technology and the microwave. At Fenway Park and in many other stadiums, an automatic conveyor belt carries hot dogs, already "bunned" and wrapped through three microwave ovens heating them to 150 degrees. They are then sold the traditional way with vendors crying "Hot Dogs!" to all those fans who believe that a hot dog is a vital part of experiencing a day at the ballpark.

As you can see from these two paragraphs, the topic sentence is not always clearly stated. This is especially true in a number of the convoluted textbooks all of us have read. When trying to discern the main idea of such writing, you may need a more in-depth analysis.

You can begin your analysis by turning, once again, to our helpful questions. Is the passage written to address one of the questions?

1. *Who?* The paragraph focuses on a particular person or group of people. The topic sentence tells you *who* this is.

2. *When?* The paragraph is primarily concerned with *time*. The topic sentence may even begin with the word "when."

3. *Where?* The paragraph is oriented around a particular place or location. The topic sentence states *where* you are reading about.

4. *Why?* A paragraph that states reasons for some belief or happening usually addresses this question. The topic sentence answers *why* something is true or *why* an event happened.

5. *How?* A paragraph that identifies the way something works or the means by which

something is done. The topic sentence explains the *how* of what is described.

You will notice that I didn't include the question "What?" in this list. This is not an oversight! "What" is not included because it addresses such a broad range of possibilities that asking this question will not necessarily lead you to the topic sentence.

The best test to determine whether you have identified the topic sentence is to rephrase this sentence as a question. If the paragraph answers the question that you've framed, you've found the topic sentence.

Summary, support or transitional?

Another technique that will lead you to the topic sentence is to identify what purpose *other* sentences in the paragraph serve, kind of a process of elimination.

Generally, sentences can be characterized as *summary, support* or *transitional*.

Summary sentences state a general idea or concept. As a rule, topic sentences are summary sentences—a concise yet inclusive statement that expresses the general intent of the paragraph. (By definition, the topic sentence is never a support sentence.)

Support sentences are those that provide the specific details and facts that give credibility to the author's points of view. They give examples, explain arguments, offer evidence, or attempt to prove something as true or false. They are not meant to state generally what the author wants to communicate—they are intended to be specific, not conceptual, in nature.

Transitional sentences move the author from one point to another. They may be viewed as a bridge connecting the paragraphs in a text, suggesting the relationship between what you just finished reading and what you are about to read.

Good readers are attuned to the signals such sentences provide—they are buzzers that scream, "This is what you are going to find out next!"

Transitional sentences may also alert you to what you should have just learned. Unlike support sentences, transitional sentences provide invaluable and direct clues to what the topic sentence is.

Some examples of transitional signals

Any sentence that continues a progression of thought or succession of concepts is a transitional sentence. Such a sentence may begin with a word such as "First," "Next," "Finally," or "Then" and indicate the before/after connection between changes, improvements or alterations. Transitional sentences that begin in this way should raise these questions in your mind:

1. Do I know what the previous examples were?
2. What additional example am I about to learn?
3. What was the situation prior to the change?

Other transition statements suggest a change in argument or thought or an exception to a rule. These will generally be introduced by words like "But," "Although," "Though," "Rather," "However" or similar conjunctions that suggest an opposing thought. Such words ought to raise these questions:

1. What is the gist of the argument I just read?
2. What will the argument I am about to read state?
3. To what rule is the author offering an exception?

In your effort to improve your reading, developing the ability to recognize the contrast between general, inclusive words and statements (summary sentences) and specific, detail-oriented sentences (transitional or support sentences) is paramount.

Taking Notes

The final step toward grasping and retaining the main idea of any paragraph is taking notes. There are several traditional methods students employ—outlining, highlighting, mapping and drawing a concept tree.

An exhaustive review of all these methods is impossible in the few pages I have here. For a complete discussion of note-taking, be sure to read *Take Notes*, another of the five books in my **HOW TO STUDY** *Program.*

Whichever method you employ to retain the main idea, focus on the topic sentences, not on the specific details.

If you are a highlighter—you enjoy coloring textbooks with fluorescent markers—you will want to assign one color that you will always use to highlight topic sentences. Avoid what too many students do—highlighting virtually every paragraph. This practice will just extend your review time considerably—you'll find yourself re-reading instead of reviewing.

If you utilize outlining or mapping—diagramming what you read rather than spending time worrying about Roman numerals and whether to use lower case letters or upper case letters—you will find that your time will best be spent writing five-word summaries of the topic sentences. If you find yourself getting bogged down in details and specifics, you are wasting valuable time. Again, writers are using these details to communicate their concepts— not necessarily to be remembered.

Read the following passage from an economics text, seeking out the topic sentences. Then summarize the main idea or ideas in five-word phrases.

The Real Economy and Worldwide Capital

Investments by rich Americans do not any longer "trickle down" to the rest of the population. Instead, they flow out into the world at large, seeking the best returns available.

At the same time, foreigners' investments seek good returns in the United States. Investments from overseas had risen to $2 trillion in 1989, an increase of 12 percent from the prior year. Since 1980, the U.S. has seen a fourfold increase in foreign capital investment. Capital moves around the world, paying little or no attention to borders.

Similarly, American money goes abroad as U.S. firms looking for higher profits build factories, buy equipment, and establish laboratories in foreign countries. As a result, although profits earned in the United States by American multi-national corporations fell 19 percent in 1989, foreign profits at these same firms increased by 14 percent.

Therefore, wealthy American citizens might enjoy high returns from their foreign investments, but few other Americans enjoy the results. Simply put, the cohesion between American capitalists and the American economy is becoming unglued.

Do your summaries resemble these?

1. Rich Americans invest more abroad
2. No more trickle-down to population
3. Foreign investment in U.S. up
4. American investments down here, up abroad
5. Little connection between wealthy Americans and American economy

I didn't always keep my summaries to five words, but I distilled the main ideas to the fewest words I could.

Nor did I always write one summary statement per paragraph, just what was needed to capture the main idea or ideas from each paragraph.

As you review my summary statements, you'll also notice that I didn't include any specific details—no numbers, no dates. Summary statements are only to identify the main ideas. The details will follow.

Chapter 4

Gathering The Facts

Now, what I want is Facts. Teach these boys and girls nothing but Facts. Facts alone are wanted in life. Plant nothing else, and root out everything else. You can only form the minds of reasoning animals upon Facts: nothing else will ever be of any service to them. This is the principle on which I bring up my own children, and this is the principle on which I bring up these children. Stick to Facts, sir!

—Charles Dickens, *Hard Times*

Seeking out the facts, as Dickens's character would have us do, is also an effective way to confront your classroom reading assignments.

While such a "just the facts, ma'am" approach is not the whole formula for scholastic success, you'll find that the vast majority of your assigned reading requires a thorough recall of the facts.

In the previous chapter, we discussed the "forest"—the main idea. In this chapter, we will concentrate on "the trees"—how to read to gather facts, the specific details that support and develop the author's main point.

Facts: Building blocks for ideas

Facts are the building blocks that give credibility to concepts and ideas. Your ability to gather and assimilate these facts will dramatically enhance your success at remembering what the author wanted to communicate.

If, however, you spend so much time studying the trees that you lose sight of the forest, your reading effectiveness will be limited. You must learn to discern what facts are salient to your understanding, and which ones to leave for the next Trivial Pursuit update.

If you are trying to identify your purpose for reading this chapter, it's twofold:

1. To develop the skill of skimming a text for facts as quickly as possible
2. To distinguish between an important detail and a trivial one

Deciphering the message

The author of any kind of writing should have something to say, a message to communicate.

Unfortunately, such messages are often lost in the glut of verbiage many authors use to "dress up" their basic point. It's your job to rake through the mess and get to the heart of the text.

You need to approach each reading assignment with the mind-set of Sherlock Holmes (or Joe Friday, if you prefer): There is a mystery to be solved, and you are the master detective. The goal is to figure out what the text is trying to communicate—regardless of how deeply it is buried in the quagmire of convoluted language.

What is the message?

The first step in any good investigation is to collect all the clues. What are the facts? By spending a few minutes of your time discerning these concrete facts, you will be far better equipped to digest what it is the author is trying to communicate.

But how do you extract the facts when they appear to be hidden in an impenetrable forest of words? You may need a little help—from "who-what-when-where-why-and-how." It seems that the facts readily sally forth when these six trusty questions are called upon the scene.

Exercise: Read the following excerpt, keeping these six words in mind. After you have finished reading it, answer the questions that follow, *without* referring back to the text.

When told to communicate, most people immediately think of writing or speaking — verbal communication. Yet, there is another form of communication that everyone uses— without realizing it. Through various facial expressions, body movements and gestures, we all have a system of nonverbal communication.

We constantly signal to others our feelings and attitudes unconsciously through actions we may not even realize we are performing. One type is called barrier signals. Since most people usually feel safer behind a barrier, they often unthinkingly fold their arms or find some other pretext for placing their arms in front of their body when they feel insecure.

Such nonverbal communication can lead to serious misunderstanding if you are not careful. Take the simple symbol you make by forming a circle with your thumb and forefinger. In America it means "OK." In France, however, it signifies a zero, something—or someone—worthless. Imagine the offense a French waiter might take if you signified your satisfaction with your meal with this sign! You would offend and insult when you only intended to praise.

1. One type of unconcious nonverbal communication is:
   A. Barrier signals
   B. Barrow signals
   C. Barrator signals
   D. Barter signals

2. Communicating through body signals is often:
   A. Nonverbal
   B. Conscious
   C. Unconscious
   D. Unnoticeable

3. Through facial expressions and body movements, we communicate:
   A. Attitudes and emotions
   B. Facts and figures
   C. Praise or insults
   D. Friendship

4. People fold their arms when they feel:
   A. Insecure
   B. Disillusioned

C. Depressed

D. Ecstatic

5. The thumb-forefinger symbol is an insult to:

   A. The French

   B. Europeans

   C. Americans

   D. Waiters

In the preceding exercise, you should have quickly read through the text and been able to answer all five questions. If it took you more than three minutes to do so, you spent too much time. You were reading *only* to answer our six questions—who?, what?, when?, where?, why? and how? Your purpose was to get to the facts, nothing more.

(The correct answers, by the way, are all "A's"...just what mastery of this book will lead to!)

Skimming defined

What is skimming? Skimming is the technique we all employ when using the phone book—unless, of course, you're in the habit of reading every name in the book to find the one you're looking for. When you skim, your eyes do not look at every word, read every sentence or think about every paragraph. Instead, they rapidly move across the page to find just what you are looking for and then read that carefully.

When I was in college, I would begin any assignment by reading the first sentence of every paragraph and trying to answer the questions at the chapter's end. If this did not give me a pretty good idea of the content and important details of that chapter, then—and only then— would I read it more thoroughly.

I'm sure this method of skimming for the facts saved me countless hours of time (and boredom).

Ask first, then look

When skimming for detail, you will often have a particular question, date or fact you need to find. You should approach the text much like the dictionary— knowing the word, you just skim the pages to find its definition. If you must answer a specific question or read about a historic figure, you simply find a source—book, magazine or encyclopedia—and quickly skim the text for the answer or person.

You probably are assigned a lot of reading that can be accomplished by skimming for facts. By establishing the questions you want answered *before* you begin to read, you can quickly browse through the material, extracting only the information you need.

Let's say you're reading a U.S. History text with the goal of identifying the key players in the Watergate Affair. You can breeze through the section that paints a picture of the day's political scene. You can whizz through the description of the Watergate Towers. And you can briefly skim the highlights of other questionable and clandestine political activity in the American past. You *know* what--or who--you're looking for. And there they are—Chuck Colson, John Dean, Mitchell, Liddy. The whole gang. Now you can start to *read.*

By identifying the questions you wanted to answer *(aka* your purpose) in advance, you would be able to skim the chapter and answer your questions--in a lot less time than it would have taken to painstakingly read every word.

As a general rule, if you are reading textbook material word for word, you probably are wasting quite a bit of your study time. Good readers are able to discern what they should read in this manner and what they can afford to skim. When trying to simply gather detail and facts, skimming a text is a simple and very important shortcut. Within minutes, you want to be able to skim the entire assignment and have a general idea of what is in it. Your ability to skim a chapter—even something you need to read more critically—will enable you to develop a general sense of what the chapter is about and how thoroughly it needs to be read.

Exercise: Answer the following questions by skimming the paragraph that follows.

1. How many days are in an astronomical year?
2. Calendar years have how many days? Hours? Minutes? Seconds?
3. To regain the fraction of a day lost each calendar year, what is done?

> Why do we have leap years? They occur to make up the day lost by the fact that our calendar year and the astronomical year do not coincide exactly. An astronomical year has 2,424 days. In calendar years, this is 365 days, five hours, 45 minutes, and twelve seconds. The extra fraction of a day is made up by what we call leap years— when we add an extra day to February. This is done to keep our calendar year in step with the seasons, which are based on the astronomical year.

If this were part of your assigned reading, you would be finished when you had answered the questions. "But I didn't read it," you protest. Can you write a one-sentence summary of the paragraph? If you *can*, and you answered the questions correctly, then you know all you need to.

Skimming, or pre-reading, is a valuable step even if you aren't seeking specific facts. When skimming for a general overview, there's a very simple procedure to follow:

1. If there is a title or heading, *rephrase it as a question.* This will be your purpose for reading.

2. Examine all the *subheadings, illustrations, and graphics,* as these will help you identify the significant matter within the text.

3. Read thoroughly the *introductory paragraphs,* the summary at the end and any questions at the chapter's end.

4. Read the *first sentence* of every paragraph. As we found in Chapter 3, this is generally where the main idea of a text is found.

5. *Evaluate* what you have gained from this process: Can you answer the questions at the end of the chapter? Could you intelligently participate in a class discussion of the material?

6. *Write* a brief summary that encapsulizes what you have learned from your skimming.

7. Based on this evaluation, *decide* whether a more thorough reading is required.

Exercise: Let's see how well you can skim for an overview, rather than for specific facts. Read the following passage, then follow the seven steps outlined above:

Democrats Vs. Republicans: The Real Economy

The cornerstone of Republican economics is that the entire population benefits when the rich are permitted to retain more of their income for themselves. Former President Ronald Reagan believed the benefits enjoyed by wealthy Americans as a result of the 1981 tax cut would "trickle down" to all other citizens. Similarly, President George Bush has advocated lowering the tax on capital gains. This would benefit the wealthy, who own most of the nation's assets, and, he contends, give a boost to the economy that would help the common man, too.

The Democrats, on the other hand, contend that such a distribution of the tax burden is unfair. They think the federal government should increase taxes for wealthy citizens, and that government should spread the wealth directly through a variety of social programs.

The two sides were in a classic standoff through the 1980s. The Republicans were successful in keeping taxes on the wealthy low, while the Democrats did their best to ensure that spending on social programs stayed high. Since members from both camps thought it wise to increase military expenditures during the decade, the federal budget had nowhere to go but up.

In the budget agreement struck between Dem-ocrats and Republicans in 1990, both sides gave in a little. Taxes on the rich will increase a bit, and social, or entitlement, programs will grow when the government can pay the bills.

But at the heart of this compromise, which is more like a cease-fire rather than a treaty to end the long war, legislators face the same choices: growth or fairness, private investment or public spending, tax cuts for the wealthy or entitlement programs for the middle class and poor. In this war, the Republicans wave the flag of pure American capitalism, with its ideals of individualism and self-determination. The Democrats, some would argue, represent the kinder, gentler side of human nature.

> But is this the real choice facing Americans in the 1990s and beyond? Many would argue that it is not. And the reason is that both sides are wrong. The American capitalism so dear to the Republicans is no longer dependent on the private investments of motivated, aggressive American capitalists. Future economic success in the United States depends instead on the country's unique qualities: the skills and insights of the workforce and their application to the realities of a global economy.
>
> The Democrats are equally wrong: The role of government is not merely to spread the wealth. It is to build "human capital" and our infrastructure. More than ever, brain power, linked by roads, airports, computers, and cables, is the key factor in determining a nation's standard of living.

While it may not be evident at first, you'll soon see how skimming can save you a lot of reading time. Even if a more in-depth reading is necessary, you will find that by having gone through this process, you will have developed the kind of skeletal framework that will make your further reading faster, easier and more meaningful.

You will have equipped yourself with the ability to better digest what it is the author is trying to communicate.

Chapter 5

The Challenge Of Technical Texts

You've already learned a lot of ways to improve your reading. It's time to examine the unique challenges posed by highly technical texts. Physics, trigonometry, chemistry, calculus—you know, subjects that three-fourths of all students avoid like the plague. Even those students who manage to do well in such subjects wouldn't dare call them "Mickey Mouse" courses.

More than any other kind of reading, these subjects demand a logical, organized approach, a step-by-step reading method.

And they require a detection of the text's *organizational devices*

Developing the skill to identify the basic sequence of the text will enable you to follow the progression of thought, a progression that is vital to your comprehension and retention.

Why?

In most technical writing, each concept is a like a building block of understanding—if you don't understand a particular section or concept, you won't be able to understand the *next* section, either.

Most technical books are saturated with ideas, terms, formulas and theories. The chapters are dense with information, compressing a great wealth of ideas into a small space. They demand to be read very carefully.

In order to get as much as possible from such reading assignments, you can take advantage of some devices to make sense of the organization. Here are five basic to watch for:

1. Definitions and terms
2. Examples
3. Classifications and listings
4. Use of contrast
5. Cause-effect relationships

As you read any text, but certainly highly specialized ones, identifying these devices will help you grasp the main idea, as well as any details that are essential to your thorough understanding of the material.

Definitions and terminology

In reading any specialized text, you must begin at the beginning—understanding the terms particular to that discipline. Familiar, everyday words have very precise definitions in technical writing.

What do I mean? Take the word *nice*. You may compliment your friend's new sweater, telling her it's *nice,* meaning attractive. You may find that the new chemistry teacher is *nice*, meaning he doesn't give too much homework. And when your friend uses the word *nice* to describe the blind date she's set up for you, it may mean something completely different—and insidious. Everyday words can have a variety of meanings, some of them even contradictory, depending on the context in which they're used.

In contrast, in the sciences, terminology has fixed and specific meanings. For example, the definition of elasticity—*'the ability of a solid to regain its shape after a deforming force has been applied"*—is the same in Bangkok or Brooklyn. Such exact terminology enables scientists to communicate with the kind of precision their discipline requires.

Definitions may vary in length. One term may require a one-sentence definition, others merit entire paragraphs. Some may even need a whole chapter to accurately communicate the definition.

Examples help clarify the abstract

A second communication tool is the example. Authors use such examples to bridge abstract principles to concrete illustrations. These examples are essential to your ability to comprehend intricate and complicated theories.

Unlike other writing, technical writing places a very high premium on brevity. Economizing words is the key to covering a large volume of knowledge in a relatively short space. Few technical texts or articles include anecdotal matter or chatty stories of the author's experience.

This fact challenges the reader to pay particular attention to the examples that are included. Why? Technical writing often is filled with new or foreign ideas—many of which are not readily digestible. They are difficult in part because they are abstract. Examples work to clarify these concepts, hopefully in terms more easily understood. For example, it may be difficult for you to make sense of the definition for symbiosis—*"the living together of two dissimilar organisms, especially when mutually beneficial"*—but the example of the bird that picks food from the crocodile's teeth, thereby feeding itself and keeping the crocodile cavity-free, helps bring it home.

Classification and listings

A third tool frequently utilized in texts is classification and listings. Classifying is the process by which subjects that are common are categorized under a general heading.
Some examples:

Matter may occur in three forms: solid, liquid or gas.

Classification: Three forms of matter

Listing: Solid, liquid, gas

The social sciences are psychology, economics, and sociology

Classification: Social sciences

Listing: Psychology, economics, sociology

Especially in technical writing, authors use classification to categorize extensive lists of detail. Such writings may have several categories and subcategories that organize these details into some manageable fashion.

Comparing/Contrasting

A fourth tool used in communicating difficult information is that of comparing and contrasting. Texts use this tool to bring complicated material into focus by offering an opposing picture or one that is similar.

Such devices are invaluable in grasping concepts that do not conjure a picture in your mind. Gravity, for example, is not something that can be readily pictured—it's not a tangible, touchable object that can be described.

Through comparison, a text relates a concept to one that has been previously defined—or to one a reader may readily understand. Through contrast, the text concentrates on the differences and distinctions between two ideas. By focusing on distinguishing features, these ideas become clearer as one idea is held up against another.

Cause-effect relationships

A final tool that texts employ to communicate is that of cause-effect relationships. This device is best defined in the context of science ,where it is the fundamental quest of most scientific research.

Science begins with the observation of the effect—what is happening?

It is snowing.

The next step is to conduct research into the cause: *Why* is it snowing? Detailing this cause-effect relationship is often the essence of scientific and technical writing.

Cause-effect relationships may be written in many ways. The effect may be stated first, followed by the cause. An effect may be the result of several connected causes—a causal chain. And a cause may have numerous effects.

In your reading, it is vital that you recognize this relationship and its significance.

Read with a plan

More than any other type of writing, highly specialized, technical writing must be read with a plan. You

can't approach your reading assignment merely with the
goal of completing it. Such mindless reading will leave
you confused and frustrated, drowning in a quagmire of
theory, concepts, terms and examples.

Your plan should incorporate the following guide-
lines:

1. *Learn the terms* that are essential to
   understanding the concepts presented.
   Knowing the precise definitions that the
   author uses will enable you to follow his
   chain of thought through the text.

2. *Determine the structure or organization
   of the text.* Most chapters have a definite
   pattern that forms the skeleton of the material. A book may begin with a statement
   of a theory, give examples, provide sample
   problems, then summarize. Often this
   pattern can be discerned through a pre-
   view of the table of contents or the titles
   and subtitles.

3. *Skim the chapter* to get a sense of the
   author's viewpoint. Ask questions to define your purpose in reading. Use any
   summaries or review questions to guide
   your reading.

4. Do a *thorough, analytical reading* of the
   text. Do not proceed from one section to
   the next until you have a clear understanding of the section you are reading.
   The concepts generally build upon each
   other. To proceed to a new section without
   understanding the ones that precede it is,
   at best, futile.

5. Immediately upon concluding your thorough reading, *review!* Write a summary of the concepts and theories you need to remember. Answer any questions raised when you skimmed of the text. Do the problems. If possible, apply the formulas.

Technical material is saturated with ideas. When reading it, you must be convinced of one fact: Every word counts! You will want to read such material with the utmost concentration—it is not meant to be sped through.

Good readers know that such material demands a slow read that concentrates on achieving the greatest level of retention.

Every definition has to be digested.

Every formula committed to memory.

Every example considered.

To improve your reading of such technical material you will want to hone the skill of identifying the devices an author uses to communicate. In so doing, you will be able to connect the chain of thought that occurs.

Chapter 6

Becoming A Critical Reader

Analyze and interpret the following statements:

How The Art Of Reasoning Is Necessary

When one of his audience said, "Convince me that logic is useful," he said, "Would you have me demonstrate it?"

"Yes."

"Well, then, must I not use a demonstrative argument?"

And, when the other agreed, he said, "How then shall you know if I impose upon you?"

And when the man had no answer, he said, "You see how you yourself admit that logic is necessary, if without it you are not even able to learn this much—whether it is necessary or not."

In a republican nation, whose citizens are to be led by reason and persuasion and not by force, the art of reasoning becomes of first importance."

— Thomas Jefferson

Anyway, I keep picturing all these little kids playing some game in this big field of rye and all. Thousands of little kids, ald nobody's around—nobody big, I mean, except me. And I'm standing on the edge of some crazy cliff. What I have to do, I have to catch everybody if they start to go over the cliff—I mean if they're running and they don't look where they're going I have to come out from somewhere and catch them. That's all I'd do all day. I'd just be the catcher in the rye..."

— Excerpt from J.D. Salinger, *Catcher In The Rye*

He who has a why to live can bear with almost any how."

— Nietzsche

After four years of undergraduate work, before my dear alma mater would award me the degree for which I felt my dollars, sweat and blood had amply paid, I was made to endure a six-hour essay test that began much like your instructions here. We literature majors were given one question—"Analyze and interpret the following:" The "following" being a poem we had never seen before...and several blue books in which to write our erudite answers.

Unbelievable?

Hardly!

This test was given in much the same way that the Educational Testing Service gives their PSAT, SAT, LSAT and GMAT verbal tests. In the notorious reading comprehension section, you are required to read a distilled passage—which, unless you've stolen a peek at the exam, you have never seen—and then given four to six questions to determine if you have any clue as to what you just read. You will find that there are many times, particularly in comparative literature classes, when you will need to read something with great care in order to remember details and interpret meaning. Hester Prynne's red monogram, Poe's talking raven and Ponzo's and Lucky's mysterious friend all require a little more analysis than a superficial interpretation of props and plot.

Yet such detailed, analytical reading is not limited to literature. Political dissertations, historical analysis and even scientific research may each require more careful reading than the latest "space opera."

Such reading is often referred to as *critical reading,* a type of reading during which you seek to distinguish thoughts, ideas or concepts—each demanding thorough study and evaluation.

Critical reading requires that you are able to identify the author's arguments, measure their worth and truth and apply what is pertinent to your own experience. Unlike skimming, critical reading challenges the reader to concentrate at the highest level possible.

Prepare yourself to read critically

When preparing to read critically, you must lay the groundwork for concentration. Just as an athlete must ready himself mentally to achieve peak performance, you will want to ready yourself before you begin to read.

The following suggestions will help you prepare to read critically:

1. You must have a clearly defined purpose for reading. Make sure that you've identified your purpose before you begin.

2. Pay attention! Avoid letting your mind wander to that conversation you and your friend had today at lunch. Minimize distractions and interruptions—anything or anyone that causes you to break your focus.

3. Find your optimum study environment— a quiet corner in the library, your own room, wherever. In absolute silence, or with your new CD playing. (Be sure to read *Manage Your Time*, another of the five books in my **HOW TO STUDY** *Program*, for more tips on finding *your* perfect study environment.)

4. Don't worry about how fast or slowly you read. Your goal should be to understand the material, not to find out "How fast can I get this over with?"

5. If it seems that you will need several hours to complete your reading, you might break the longer assignments into smaller, more manageable, parts, then reward yourself at the end of each of these sections by taking brief breaks.

If you take these steps prior to reading any text that requires your utmost concentration, you will find that your mind is readied for the kind of focus necessary to read critically. Make a *habit* of such preparations, and you will set yourself up to succeed.

Pre-reading is a must

Once you have prepared your mind to read, the next step is to understand the "big picture"—what is the author's thesis or main idea? Good comprehension is the consequence of your ability to grasp the main point of what the author is trying to communicate. Grasping this message is accomplished through skimming, as we discussed in Chapter 4. Let's review the basic steps:

1. If there is a title or heading, rephrase it as a question. This will support your purpose for reading.

2. Examine all the subheadings, illustrations and graphics, as these will help you identify the significant matter within the text.

3. Read the introductory paragraphs, the summary and any questions at the end of the chapter.

4. Read the first sentence of every paragraph. In Chapter 3, you learned that this is generally where the main idea is found.

5. Evaluate what you have gained from this process: Can you answer the question's at the chapter's end? Could you intelligently participate in a class discussion of the material?

6. Write a brief summary of what you have learned from your skimming.

By beginning your critical reading with a 20-minute "skim" of the text, you should be ready to answer three questions:

1. What is the text's principal message or viewpoint?

2. Is an obvious chain of thought or reasoning revealed?

3. What major points are addressed?

Now, *read* it

Once you identify and understand the basic skeleton of the material, your actual "read" of the material—following the details, reasoning, and chain of thought—is simply a matter of attaching meat to the bones.

This digestive process involves learning to interpret and evaluate what is written, what is directly stated and what can be inferred from the context.

Effective analytical reading requires that you, the reader, distinguish the explicit, literal meaning of words *(denotation)* and what suggestions or intentions are intimated by the general content *(connotation)*.

Analyzing: What the words *connote*

Words and writing have two levels of meaning that are important to the reader's comprehension.

The first level is the literal or descriptive meaning. What a word expressly *denotes*—the specific, precise definition you'd find in *Webster*.

Connotation involves this second level of meaning— that which incorporates the total *significance* of the words.

What does that mean?

Beyond a literal definition, words communicate emotion, bias, attitude, and perspective. Analyzing any text involves learning to interpret what is implied, just as much as what is expressly stated.

The following brainteasers challenge you to read beyond what is expressly stated.

Bill is being imprisoned by terrorists in a building that has triple locks on the door. The walls are steel-reinforced concrete and the floor is packed earth. In the middle of the ceiling, well above Bill's head is an air vent just wide enough for a man to squeeze through. There is nothing in the room for Bill to stand on to reach the vent. One night well after dark Bill escapes. How?

Matt and Candie are having a very serious game of golf—the loser buys dinner. Late in the game, with the score very close, Matt's ball rolls inside a paper bag that has been left on the course. Rules prohibit Matt from touching the bag or removing the ball from the bag. Candie insists that he not break the rule. What can Matt do to get a clear shot on his ball?

Personally, I hate brainteasers, but they are nothing compared to some of the books I was required to read in school. Textbooks, literature, and many of your reading assignments will be just as convoluted as these questions (even though their authors have not, we are assured, gone out of their way to make their books so obtuse on purpose). You will greatly increase your comprehension as you read for implicit meaning and for inference.

(Oh, you want the answers to the brainteasers? In the first one, Bill escaped from his cell by digging a hole in the packed-earth floor and climbing on top of the pile of earth to reach the vent. In the second brainteaser, Matt simply lit a match and burned the bag around his golf ball. Did you guess them?)

15 questions to help you

Beyond grasping the meaning of words and phrases, critical reading requires that you ask questions. Here are 15 questions that will help you effectively analyze and interpret most of what you read.

1. Is there a clear message communicated throughout?
2. Are the relationships between the points direct and clear?
3. Is there a relationship between your experience and the author's?
4. Are the details factual?
5. Are the examples and evidence relevant?
6. Is there consistency of thought?
7. What is the author's bias or slant?
8. What is the author's motive?
9. What does the author want you to believe?
10. Does this jibe with your own belief or experience?
11. Is the author rational or subjective?
12. Is there a confusion between feelings and facts?
13. Are the main points logically ordered?
14. Are the arguments and conclusions consistent?
15. Are the explanations clear?

Obviously, this list of questions is not all inclusive. But, it will give you a jumpstart when critical reading is required. Remember, the essential ingredient to any effective analysis and interpretation is the questions you ask.

Summarizing: The final step

The final step in any critical reading is that of summarizing. Nothing will be more important to your recall than learning to condense what you read into a clear and concise summary.

Many of you have learned to do this by excerpting entire segments or sentences from a text, certainly not a very efficient method for summarizing.

I recommend using the traditional outline (which is explained in detail in my book, *Take Notes*, yet another in my **HOW TO STUDY** *Program)*

Another suggestion is to use a two-step process called *diagramming,* which calls for the reader to *diagram* or illustrate that content that he's just read, then to write a brief synopsis of what he's learned.

Similar to outlining, diagramming helps the reader to visualize the relationships between various thoughts and ideas. Concept diagrams, or concept trees, are very useful visual aids for depicting the structure of a textbook.

Unless you have a photographic memory, you will find that recalling a picture of the main points will greatly increase what you remember. Beyond this, such diagrams require that you distill what is essential to the text and how it relates to the main message.

Suppose you read a chapter in your Biology assignment about the parts of a cell. Your diagram might reduce your reading material to look like the following:

Parts of a Cell

Outside of Cell	Inside of Cell
cell wall	cytoplasm
cell membrane	vacuoles
nucleus chloroplasts	chlorophyll

More than a listing of main points, diagrams allow you to picture how parts fit together, which enhances your ability to recall the information you've read. This is especially true the more "visual" you are.

Distill it into a synopsis

The second step in the process of summarizing is to write a brief synopsis of what you've learned. When you need to review the material, diagrams will remind you of the significant elements in the text. Your synopsis will remind you of what insight you walked away with—the main idea.

The goal here is to put in your own words what you gleaned from what you read. You will find this process of putting in your own words the author's message an invaluable gauge of whether you have understood the message —and on what level.

Critical reading is not easy. It requires a lot more concentration and effort than the quick-reference reading that you can get away with for much of your day-to-day class assignments. And I won't kid you—much of the reading you'll do in the latter years of high school and throughout college will be critical reading.

But if you follow the steps I've outlined in this chapter for each critical reading assignment that you tackle— preparing yourself for the read, doing a pre-read skim, followed by an analytical reading, concluding with a summarization—you'll discover that critical reading can be a lot smoother, even rewarding, experience!

Chapter 7

Reading The Literature

"Will you walk a little faster?" said a whiting to a snail,
"There's a porpoise close behind us and he's treading on my tail!"
"If I'd been the whiting," said Alice, whose thoughts were still running on the song, "I'd have said to the porpoise, 'Keep back, please; we don't want you with us!'"
"They were obliged to have him with them," the Mock Turtle said. "No wise fish would go anywhere without a Porpoise."
"Wouldn't it really?" said Alice in a tone of great surprise.
"Of course not," said the Mock Turtle. "Why, if a fish came to me, and told me he was going on a journey, I should say, 'With what porpoise?'"

"Don't you mean 'purpose?'"said Alice.
"I mean what I say," the Mock Turtle replied in
an offended tone.
—Lewis Carroll, *Alice in Wonderland*

In this excerpt, you could enjoy the nonsensical picture of a porpoise pushing a snail and whiting to walk faster. You might laugh at the confusion of "porpoise" and "purpose" by the Mock Turtle. Or you could discern the *message*—that you need to have a purpose when you are on a journey...or reading.

In today's world of Nintendo, Ninja Turtles and M.C. Hammer, literature often takes a back seat. So much so that many of your classmates (not *you*, of course) may not even know that *Alice in Wonderland* is an important piece of literature.

Why should you care about literature? Who needs to read the book when you can see the movie?

While I didn't write this book to give you a lecture on the merits of the classics, please bear with me for a couple of paragraphs.

The greatest involvement device

Unlike anything else, literature *involves* the reader in the story. How? There are no joysticks to manipulate, no "sensurround" sound to engulf you. Your imagination is your only involvement device, but it far surpasses any high-tech computer gimmicks.

Your imagination makes reading the ultimate adventure. It allows you to immerse yourself in the story—identifying with the protagonist, fighting his battles, experiencing his fears, sharing his victories. You may become so involved, you end up staying up well past your bedtime, turning page after page late into the night!

Your imagination is the vehicle that allows you to explore a million different lives, from floating down the Mississippi River on a raft, to suffering through a star-crossed love affair, to having tea with the March Hare and the Mad Hatter, as our Alice did.

Creative writing may be serious or humorous or sublime...or all three. It is often subtle; meanings are elusive and delicate. Such writing, when done effectively, evokes emotional responses. You get angry. You shed a tear. You chuckle. An author's expression strikes a chord that moves you. You and the author communicate on a level that is far beyond an exchange of facts and information.

Enough said. Assuming that I've converted all you literature skeptics to avid library loiterers (and even if I haven't), I'll offer some advice to help you begin your journey to literary appreciation. It begins with understanding the basic roadmap.

Which reading method? Pleasure or critical

While I certainly encourage you to approach your reading with the enthusiasm and anticipation that would justify the pleasure-reading method (see Chapter 2), the demands of your teacher who assigns the reading will probably require the *critical* reading method.

Reading literature requires most of the skills we've discussed previously.

There are devices and clues to ferret out that will help you follow the story and understand its meaning better.

You will analyze and interpret what the author is saying and evaluate its worth.

But in addition, in literature, you will be able to appreciate the *words* themselves. In textbooks, you often must penetrate a thick jungle of tangled sentences and murky paragraphs to find the information you seek.

Great literature *is* its language. It's the flow and ebb of its words, the cadence of its sentences, as much as it is story and theme.

And as you read more, you'll uncover the diversity of tapestries that different authors weave with their words. You may discover similar themes coarsing through the works of authors like Ernest Hemingway or Thomas Hardy, but their use of language is as different as desert and forest. The composition of the words themselves, then, is an element you'll want to examine as you critically read literature.

Fiction: Just another word for storytelling

Most fiction is an attempt to tell a story. There is a *beginning,* in which characters and setting are introduced. There is a *conflict or struggle* (middle) that advances the story to a *climax* (end)—where the conflict is resolved. A final denouement or "winding up" unravels or clarifies the conclusion of the story.

Your literature class will address all of these parts using literary terms that are often more confusing than helpful. The following are brief definitions of some of the more important ones:

> *Plot:* The order or sequence of the story—how it proceeds from opening through climax. Your ability to understand and appreciate literature depends upon how well you follow the plot—the *story*.

> *Characterization:* The personalities or characters central to the story—the heroes, the heroines and the villains. You will want to identify the main characters of the story and their relationship to the struggle or conflict.

Pay particular attention as to whether the characters are three dimensional—are they real and believable?

Theme: The controlling message or subject of the story, the moral or idea that the author is using the plot and characters to communicate. Some examples: man's inhumanity to man, man's impotency in his environment, the corrupting influence of power, greed and unrequited love. Just as with nonfiction, you need to discern this theme to really understand what it is the author wants to communicate.

Setting: The time and place in which the story takes place. This is especially important when reading a historical novel or one that takes you to another culture.

Point of View: Who is telling the story? Is it one of the central characters giving you flashbacks or a first-person perspective? Or is it a third-person narrator offering commentary and observations on the characters, the setting and the plot? This is the person who moves the story and gives it an overall tone.

The first step in reading literature is to familiarize yourself with these concepts—and then try to recognize them in each novel or short story you read.

The second is the same as for reading nonfiction—to identify your purpose for reading.

Allow your purpose to define how you will read. If you are reading to enjoy the story and to be entertained, then a pleasure read is the way to go. If you're reading for a class and will need to participate in discussions or know you will be tested on the material, you'll want to do a critical read.

How long should it take?

As a general rule, fiction is not meant to be read over a period of months--or even weeks. You should try to read it as quickly as possible to get a full appreciation of the author's plot, character and theme. You should read fast enough to progress through the plot, get a sense of the characters and their struggles and hear the author's message or theme.

It's helpful to set a goal as to when you want to finish your reading. Frequently, of course, this will already be set for you, if you're reading is a class assignment.

You should, however, set daily goals. Set aside one or two hours to read, or set a goal of reading three chapters a day until you finish. Reading sporadically—-10 minutes one day, a half hour the next, then not picking up the book until several days later—means that you'll lose track of the plot and characters—and just as quickly lose interest.

Too often when students do not establish a regular schedule, their reading becomes fragmented, making it very difficult to piece together the whole story. A reasonable goal is to try to read a novel in less than a week, to read a short story in one sitting. The key to achieving this goal is that once you begin, you should read every day until you finish. By doing this, the story and characters will stay fresh in your mind.

If you try to read fiction more rapidly, you will greatly increase your enjoyment of it. It is vitally important that as you try to read faster, you give the story your full attention By doing this you will be surprised by how improved your understanding and appreciation are.

To speed your reading of fiction, try this experiment:

1. Find a novel or short story that interests you and is relatively easy to read. *War and Peace* or *The Brothers Karamazov* shouldn't be candidates.

2. Set aside two or three hours to invest in reading the book. If at all possible, finish it in one sitting. If you can't, then allocate the same amount of time each day until you do.

By trying this experiment, you will discover that fiction is *intended* to be read this way—whenever possible, in one sitting.

It is as if you are sitting at a master storyteller's feet as he spins his tale. You want to know how the story ends and what happens to the hero.

Will the villain get his comeuppance? Will the hero get the girl? Or ride off with his horse?

You appreciate the story far more at the end than anywhere in the middle.

Some other tips that will help in your reading of fiction:

1. Get the plot straight and maintain awareness of its progression.

2. Take breaks to review what has occurred and who is involved.

3. Vary your reading method—from skimming transitional, bridge material to carefully reading description and narration.

4. Ask questions of the story's theme. What is the message?

You're allowed to enjoy it

A final recommendation: Give yourself permission to *enjoy* what you are reading. You will be amazed at the difference this will make. Fiction, unlike any other reading, offers to take you on an adventure. Through your mind, you can journey to faraway lands, pretend you are someone you can never be, feel emotions you may never really live.

All of this happens as you gain an appreciation of literature—as you learn to understand fiction and allow yourself to enjoy a great story.

Chapter 8

Focusing Your Mind

Concentration: It's one of the biggest challenges facing any reader.

Why? Unlike other activities, reading requires an *active* mind and a *passive* body. A deadly combination, especially when you've spent the day in classes and haven't had a chance to burn off that excess energy with a tennis game, "hoops" or a quick run around the campus.

Concentration-wise, reading can be more demanding than class lectures, doing homework assignments or taking notes. In class, you at least have vocal variety and the threat of being called on to keep you focused. And writing, while a sedentary activity, still requires some hand-eye coordination to keep your brain working.

Keep your mind on one thing

Concentration begins with the ability to keep your mind directed to one thing—your reading assignment. This is not an innate talent, but a learned discipline. Much like an athlete must learn to be so focused that he is completely uneffected by the screaming crowds, good readers absorb themselves in what they're reading.

How does *your* mind discipline "rate?" Use these questions to find out:

1. When I read, do I often allow random thoughts to steal my focus?
2. Am I easily distracted as I read by noises or other activity so that I keep looking up from my book?
3. Am I watching the clock to see how long I have read, or am I so absorbed that I'm unconcerned about time?

There is no simple, magic formula for conjuring up concentration—especially when you're faced with a critical reading assignment you're not particularly looking forward to. But if you follow the preparatory steps I've discussed in previous chapters—define your purpose, skim for a pre-read, identify questions you will seek answers for—you should find it a bit easier to stay focused.

Steps to better concentration

Here are some other practical steps I recommend to increase your ability to concentrate:

1. *Get some exercise* before you begin your reading. A game of tennis, an exercise class, a workout at the gym, even a brisk walk, will help burn off *physical* energy

so you'll be able to direct all your *mental energy* to your reading.

I knew a high school student teacher who had to face a stack of essay papers two nights a week. On those nights, she scheduled an aerobics class before she began her three-hour paper-grading session. She knew that if she didn't "feel the burn" before her work, she'd be burning the midnight oil as she struggled to stay focused.

2. **Read in the right place.** No, it's not in front of the TV, nor in your room if your roommate is hosting a pizza party. Reading is a solitary activity. Find a quiet corner, preferably in a place designated for study only—at your desk, in the library. Although tempting, reading on your bed can be dangerous if you're struggling to concentrate. You just may lose the battle and find yourself in the perfect place to doze off.

3. *Eliminate distractions.* Exercising and reading in a quiet, solitary place will help. And if you've properly scheduled your reading time (see **Manage Your Time**), you won't be distracted by other pending assignments. If you're trying to read one assignment while worrying about another, your concentration—and comprehension—will inevitably suffer.

Make sure there's nothing else in sight to vie for your attention. Letters on your desk that you need to respond to?

Put them away and schedule some time to write back. Sirens and screams from the TV show in the other room? Turn it off, down or close your door.

4. *Plan breaks.* If you have three hours or more of reading ahead of you, the mere thought of it may be so discouraging that you already can't concentrate. Schedule short 10- or 15-minute breaks, after each hour of reading. Get up. Listen to some music. Stretch or walk around. If you must break more frequently, keep your breaks shorter. By breaking up your reading into smaller, more digestible bites, you'll be able to concentrate more effectively.

Wait! Don't start reading yet.

Have you defined your purpose for reading? Yes, once again, you must have a clearly defined purpose or goal. What are you reading for? (I know we have addressed this numerous times, but spaced repetition is a very effective way to make a point.)

The point is that reading without purpose is the greatest means to getting nowhere, which is where you'll find your mind after about a half-hour.

Know why you are reading. If your teacher or professor has given you questions to answer, then you know what you're looking for. If not, ask your *own* questions, using the clues in your book (as discussed in Chapter 2).

An effective pre-read of the material should help you define your purpose and stimulate some interest in finding out more—which will result in increased concentration.

Motivation: Crucial to concentration

Motivation, as I discussed in *Manage Your Time*, is key to your success in just about any endeavor—whether it's graduating with honors, maintaining an effective time-management program or improving your reading. You can utilize all the tricks and steps I've mentioned in this chapter. But if you lack the motivation to read, you'll still find it a struggle to concetrate on your assignments.

There are two types of motivation—*intrinsic* and *extrinsic*. What's the difference?

An avid murder mystery fan, you buy stacks of paperbacks at the used bookstore and spend your free time with your nose buried in them. You love the challenge of figuring out "who did it" before you reach the end. In fact, you'd spend all weekend reading mysteries if you didn't have to complete a reading assignment for your political science class. You're not particularly interested in the topic, but your efforts on this assignment could mean you'll secure an "A" for the term. So you're determined to read the material, and "ace" the exam.

Your motivation for reading the mysteries is intrinsic—you do it because you enjoy it. You don't get any awards. You don't get paid for it.

The poli-sci reading, on the other hand, requires external motivation. You're reading it because you want to earn a high grade in class. Your reward is external—beyond the reading itself.

Whether you are intrinsically motivated to read or doing it for some external reward doesn't matter as much as the fact that you are, indeed, motivated by something! If you find it difficult to get excited about reading your economics assignment, remind yourself of how this exercise will help your grade—and get yourself externally motivated.

And if *that* doesn't get you motivated enough to read for three hours, there's nothing wrong with a little bribery. Reward yourself with something more immediate. Promise yourself that if you stay focused on your reading until it's completed, you can watch that video afterward. Or you can buy that new CD. (Be careful, though. If you need *lots* of extrinsic motivation, you could run out of money!)

The value of concentration can be summed up in one statement: Concentration is essential to comprehension. Where there is failure to focus, there will be little or no understanding.

Without concentration, you will see only words on a page.

Chapter 9

Retaining The Information

The ultimate test of your comprehension is what you remember *after* you have finished your reading—what you walk away with. As a student, most of your reading will be for classes in which, sooner or later, you'll be required to regurgitate the information you've read in some format—essay test, term paper, multiple-choice, true-false or fill-in-the-blank final.

So, beyond just being able to *complete* your reading assignments, you want to be sure you *remember* what you read.

One of my most frustrating experiences as a student occurred during a geography test in high school. It wasn't even a hard test. But as I ran down the column of fill-in-the-blank questions, one stopped me cold: "Name three mountains located in the country of Israel today that have biblical or religious significance."

How much time had I spent on that chapter on Middle Eastern geography? Mt. Sinai came to mind quickly. (My high school years preceded Israel's return of the Sinai to Egypt.)

One down, two to go. I squeezed my eyes in concentration as I attempted to conjure up the text in that chapter. It seems that I could vaguely recall a photograph of another of these mountains, but couldn't quite bring forth the name, which appeared to be buried too deeply in my brain. I groaned in frustration and the teacher gave me a reproachful look. I had read that stuff! I should have known those other two mountains! Yet, despite my commitment to my reading assignments, I just couldn't remember their names.

Well, believe me, although my memory wasn't working that day, I'll always remember the frustration I felt during that test. And I'll probably never forget that Mt. Tabor and Masada are two other mountains in Israel. (At least, they were in Israel the last time I checked.)

All of you have probably had similar experiences of forgetting that important fact that made the difference between an A-minus and a B-plus (or a B-minus and a C-plus). It was right there, on the tip of your brain. But you just couldn't quite remember it.

Memory *can* be improved

You probably know people with photographic (or near-photographic) memories. They know all the words to all the songs in *Rolling Stone's* Top Fifty, remind you of things you said to them three years ago and never forget anyone's birthday (or anniversary or "day we met" or "first kiss day," *ad infinitum.)*

While some people seem to be able to retain information naturally, a good memory—like good concentration—*can* be learned. You can control what stays in your mind and what is forgotten. The key to this control is to learn and tap into the essential elements of good memory. Some people remember with relative ease and have no problem retaining large volumes of information. Others often are aggravated by a faulty memory that seems to lose more than it retains. Several factors contribute to your capability to recall information you take in:

> *Intelligence, age and experiences* all play a role in how well you remember. People are different and not everyone remembers the same way. You need to identify how these affect your memory and learn to maximize your strengths.

> *Laying a strong foundation* is important to good memory. Most learning and memory are additions or attachments to something you have previously learned. If you never grasped basic chemistry, then mastering organic chemistry will be virtually impossible. By developing a broad base of basic knowledge, you will enhance your ability to recall new information.

> *Motivation is key* to improving your memory. A friend of mine, the consummate baseball fan, seems to know every baseball statistic from the beginning of time. He can spout off batting averages and ERAs from any decade for virtually any player—and, of course, spew out his favorite team's entire season schedule...and most of the other teams', too! While I wouldn't call him the

most intelligent guy I've ever met, he obviously loves baseball and is highly motivated to memorize as much as possible about his favorite subject.

You probably have a pet interest, too. Whether it's movies, music or sports, you've filled your brain with a mountain of information. Now, if you can learn that much about one subject, you are obviously capable of retaining information about other subjects —even chemistry. You just have to learn how to motivate yourself.

A method, system or process for retaining information is crucial to increasing your recall. This may include organizing your thinking, good study habits or mnemonic devices—some means that you utilize when you have to remember.

Using what you learn, soon after you learn it, is important to recall. It's fine to memorize a vocabulary list for a quick quiz, but if you wish to retain information "for the long haul," you must reinforce your learning by using this knowledge. For example, you will add a new word to your permanent vocabulary if you make a point to use it, correctly, in a conversation.

The study of foreign languages, for many, proves frustrating when there are no opportunities outside of class to practice speaking the language. That's why many foreign-language students join conversation groups or study abroad—to reinforce their retention of what they've learned by using it.

Why we forget

As you think about these elements in developing good memory, you can use them to address why you *forget*. At the root of poor memory is usually the failure to train yourself in one of these areas:

1. We forget when we fail to make the material meaningful.

2. We forget because we did not learn prerequisite material.

3. We forget when we fail to understand and grasp what is to be remembered.

4. We forget when the desire to remember is absent.

5. We forget when we allow apathy or boredom to dictate how we learn.

6. We forget because we have no set habit for learning.

7. We forget when we are disorganized and inefficient in our use of study time.

8. We forget because we do not use the knowledge we have gained.

All of us are inundated with information every day, bombarded with facts, concepts and opinion. We are capable of absorbing some information simply because the media drench us with it (I've never read Nancy Reagan's notorious unauthorized biography, nor do I intend to. But, how could I not be aware of her reputation for recycling Christmas gifts?).

But, in order to retain most information, we have to make a concerted effort to do so. We must make this same effort with the material we read.

How to remember

There are some basic tools that will help you remember what you read:

Understanding. You will remember only what you understand. When you read something and grasp the message, you have begun the process of retention. The test of this is your ability to state the message in your own words. Can you summarize the main idea? Unless you understand what is being said, you won't even be able to decide whether it is to be remembered or discarded.

Desire. Let me repeat: You remember what you *choose* to remember. If you do not want to retain some piece of information or don't believe you *can,* then you *won't!* To remember the material, you must *want* to remember it , and be convinced that you *will* remember it.

Overlearn. To insure that you retain material, you need to go beyond simply doing the assignment. To really remember what you learn, you should learn material thoroughly, or *over*learn. This involves pre-reading the text, doing a critical read and having some definite means of review that reinforces what you should have learned.

Systematize. It's more difficult to remember random thoughts or numbers than those organized in some pattern. For example, which phone nummber is easier to remember: 538-6284, or 678-1234? Once you recognize the pattern in the second number, it takes much less effort to remember than the first. You should develop the ability to discern the structure that exists and recall it when you try to remember. Have a system to help you recall how information is organized and connected.

Association. It's helpful to attach or associate what you are trying to recall to something you already have in your memory. Mentally link new material to existing knowledge so that you are giving this new thought some context in your mind.

If we take these principles and apply them to your reading assignment, we can develop a procedure that will increase what you take with you from your reading.

A procedure to improve recall

Each time you attempt to read something that you must recall, use this six-step process to assure that you will remember:

1. *Evaluate the material and define your purpose* for reading. Identify your interest level, and get a sense of how difficult the material is.

2. *Choose appropriate reading techniques* for the purpose of your reading. If you are reading to grasp the main idea then that is what you will recall.

3. *Identify the important facts.* Remember what you need to. Let your purpose for reading dictate what you remember, and identify associations that connect the details you must recall.

4. *Take notes.* Use your own words to give a synopsis of the main ideas. Use an outline, a diagram or a concept tree to show relationship and pattern. Your notes provide an important backup to your memory. Writing down the key points will further reinforce your ability to remember.

5. *Review.* Quiz yourself on those things you must remember. Develop some system by which you review notes at least three times before you are required to recall. The first review should be shortly after you have read; the second should come a few days later and the final review take place just before you are expected to recall. This process will help you avoid cram sessions.

6. *Implement.* Find opportunities to *use* the knowledge you have gained. Study groups and class discussions are invaluable opportunities to implement what you have learned. Participate in these—they will greatly increase what you recall.

Memorizing and mnemonics

To this point, we have concentrated on the fundamentals of remembering and retention. There are specific methods to help you recall when you must remember a lot of specific facts. The first of these is memorization—the process of trying to recall information word-for-word.

Memorize only when you are required to remember something for a relatively short time—when you have a history quiz on battle dates, a chemistry test on specific formulas or a vocabulary test in French.

When memorization is required, you should do whatever is necessary to impress the exact information on your mind. Repetition is probably the most effective method. Write down the information on a 3 X 5 card and use it as a flashcard. You must quiz yourself frequently to assure that you know the information perfectly.

A second technique for recalling lots of details is *mnemonics*. A mnemonic device is used to help recall large bits of information which may or may not be logically connected. Such mnemonics are invaluable when you must remember facts not arranged in a clear fashion, items that are quite complicated and numerous items that are a part of a series.

An example of a mnemonic device is the use of acronymns that combine the first letters from a series of words. One such acronym is used to recall the colors of the spectrum and the order in which they occur:

R	Red
O	Orange
Y	Yellow
G	Green
B	Blue
I	Indigo
V	Violet

Roy G. Biv (strange name, but memorable!) has probably gotten more elementary school kids through their science tests that can be counted.

You will find that in business or the classroom, mnemonic devices like this allow you to readily recall specific information that you need to retain for longer periods of time. They are used to remember chemical classifications, lines of music ("Every Good Boy Does Fine" is a start) and anatomical lists.

As effective as mnemonic devices are, don't try to create them for everything you have to remember. Why? To generate a device for everything you need to learn would demand more time than any one person has. And you just might have trouble *remembering* all the devices you created to help you *remember!* Too many mnemonics can make your retention more complicated and hinder effective recall.

Complex mnemonics are not very useful—they can be too difficult to memorize. When you choose to utilize a mnemonic, you should keep it simple so that it facilitates the quick recall you intended.

Many people complain that their mind is a sieve— everything they read slips through; they never remember anything.

I hope you now are convinced that this is a *correctable* problem. You don't have to be a genius to have good retention—you simply must be willing to work at gaining the skills that lead to proficient recall. As you master these skills, you will improve your reading by increasing your rate of retention.

Chapter 10

Reading: A Lifelong Activity

And further, by these, my son, be admonished: of making many books there is no end...
— Solomon (*Ecclesiastes* 12:12)

Well, you made it through another book. I hope you found the motivation—whether intrinsic or extrinsic—to define your purpose, discern the important details, grasp the main idea and retain what you read here. I promised not to preach about the joys of reading. And I haven't...too much.

Your need to read—and comprehend and retain what you read—will not end when you graduate from school.

Planning on working? From the very first week, when you're handed the company policy guide, you'll be expected to seek out the facts—like what happens if you're late more than twice.

You'll be required to read critically—and know what statements like, "Our dress code requires professional attire at all times," mean.

Business proposals, annual reports, patient charts, corporate profiles, product reports, sales reports, budget proposals, business plans, resumes, complaint letters, inter-office memos—no matter what type of work you do, you won't be able to avoid the avalanche of paper and required reading that accompanies it.

Not only will your job require the ability to read and comprehend, but so will other facets of your life. If you plan to own your home, wait 'til you see the pile of paperwork you'll have to wade through.

Credit card applications? Better read the fine print to make sure you know when your payment must be in...and how much interest you're paying on that brand-new TV.

Insurance policies, appliance warranties, local ordinances, newspapers, membership applications, and tax forms—it seems like any goal you pursue in your life will require you to scale mountains of reading material.

For your own best interest, you must be prepared to read—and understand.

I wish you the greatest possible success in your future reading pursuits, of which there will be many...throughout your life.

Index

Improve Your Reading